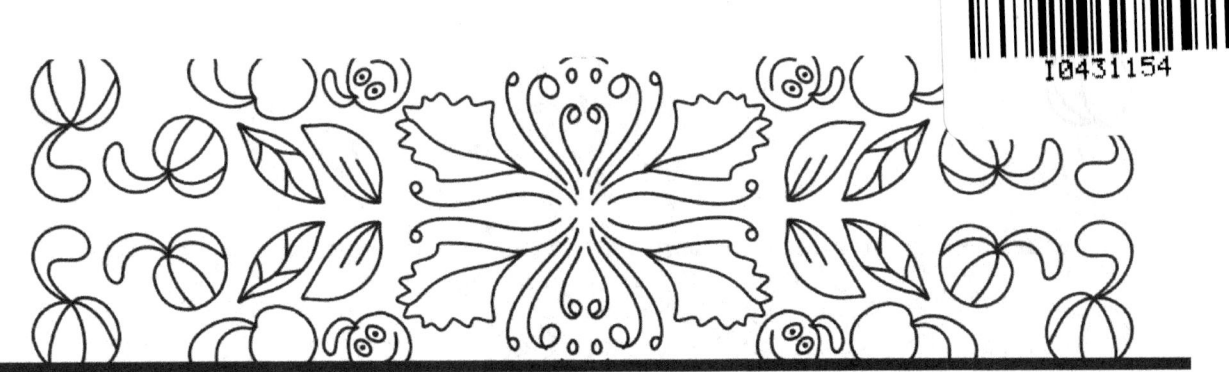

BOOKMARKS COLORING BOOK

125 Hand drawn Designs

Smita Keisser

THIS BOOK BELONGS TO

_____

_____

_____

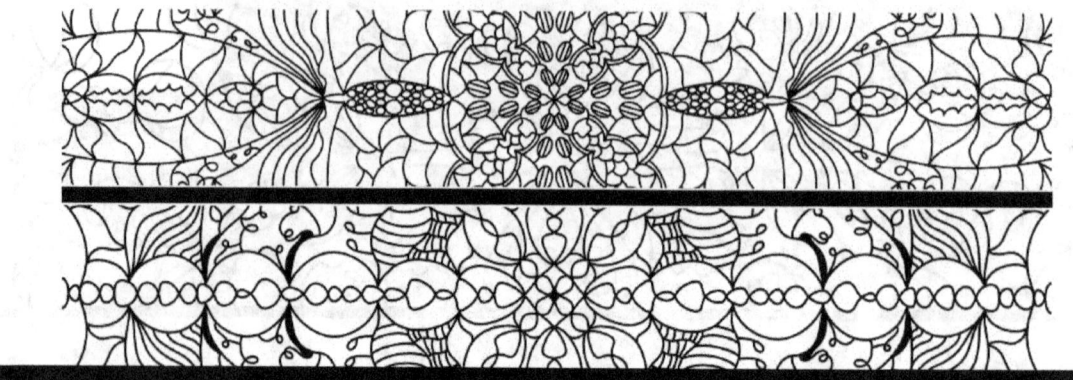

THANK YOU FOR YOUR INTEREST IN MY ART DESIGN BOOKMARKS
THESE ARE MY HAND DRAWN ART
SOME ARE VERY SIMPLE SO THAT KIDS CAN JOIN IN TO COLOR
OTHERS ARE VERY INTRICATE
SOMETHING FOR EVERY ONE IN THE FAMILY
TREAT IT AS A COLORING BOOK OR
CUT THEM OUT TO LAMINATE THEM AS PAPER IS NOT THICK CARD STOCK QUALITY

I HOPE TO INSPIRE YOU
AND
ENJOY COLORING!

FEEL FREE TO LEAVE A REVIEW

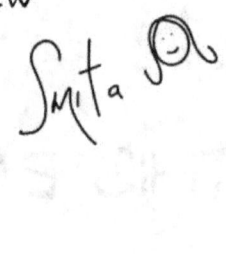

©2022 copyright Smita Keisser All rights reserved
This book may not be reproduced or transmitted in any form or by any means
electronic or mechanical without written permission from the author.

smitakeisser.com

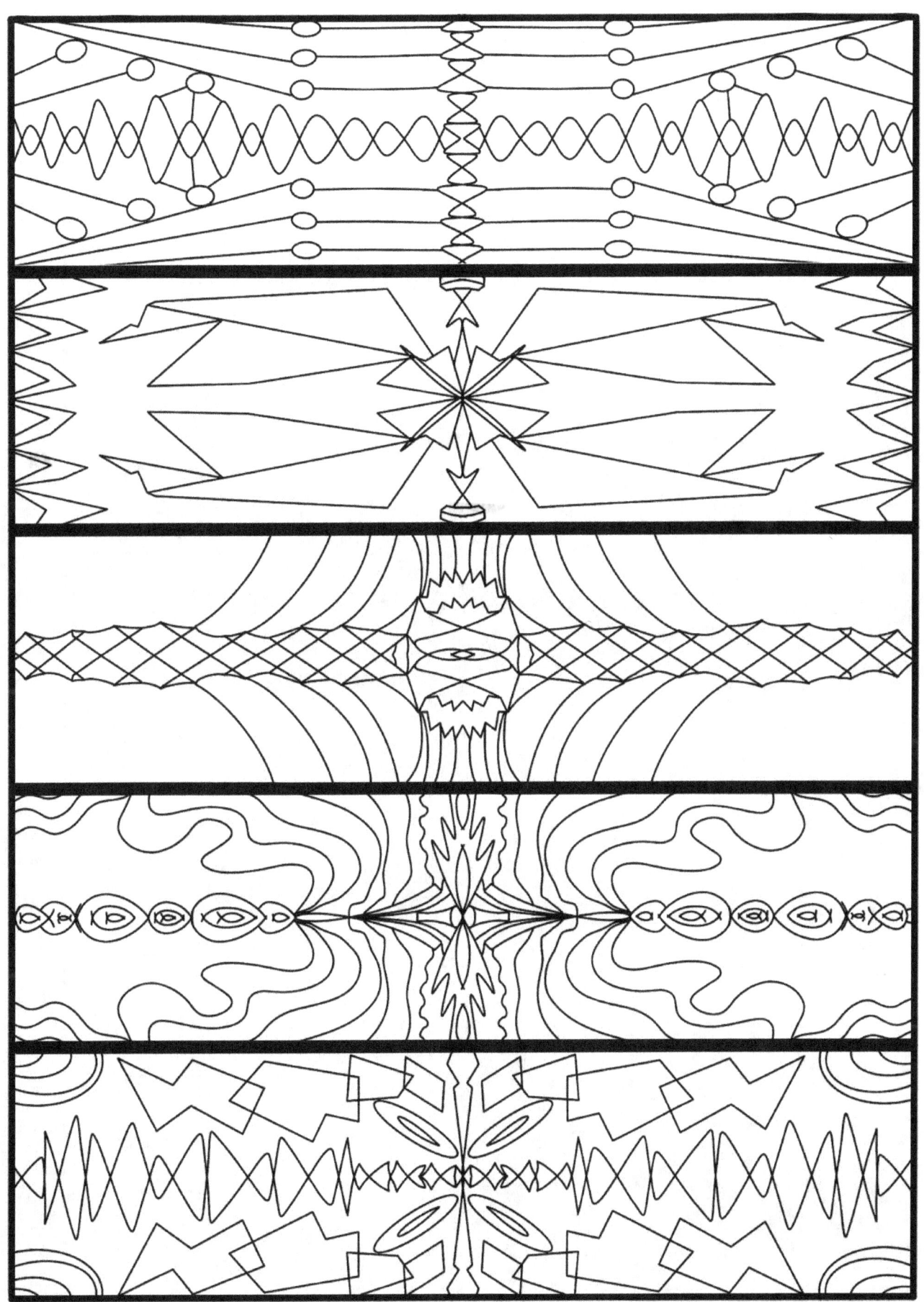

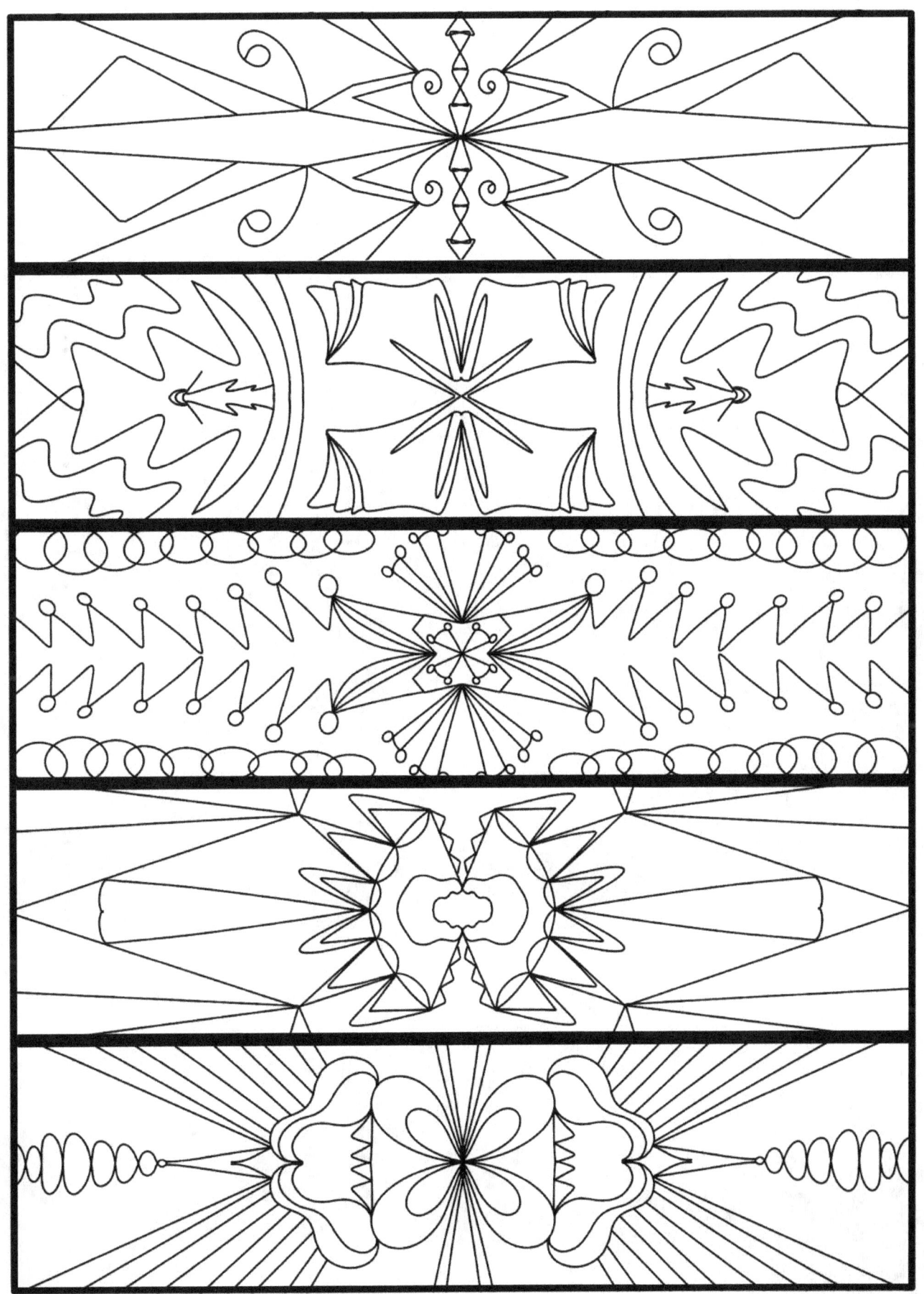

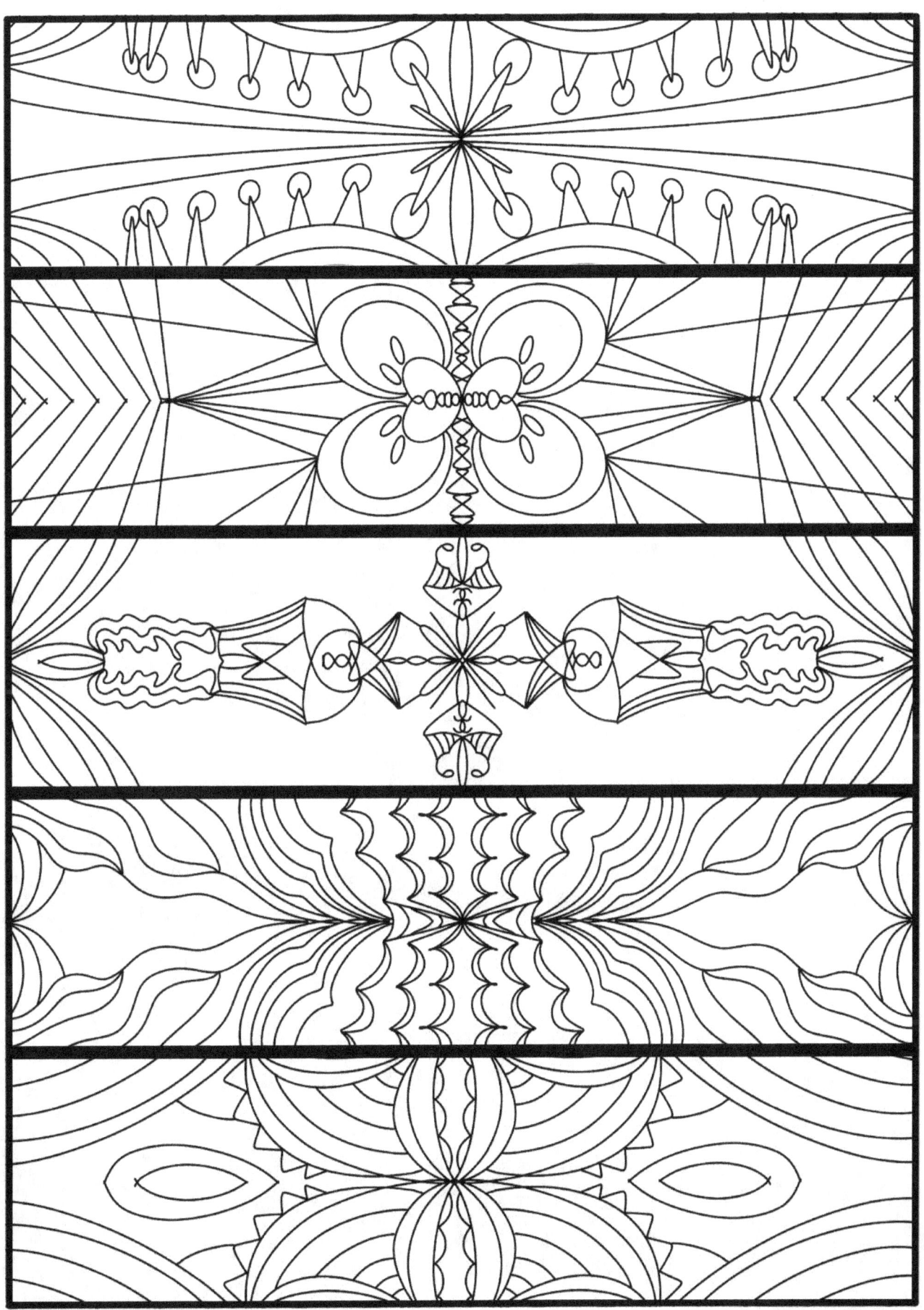

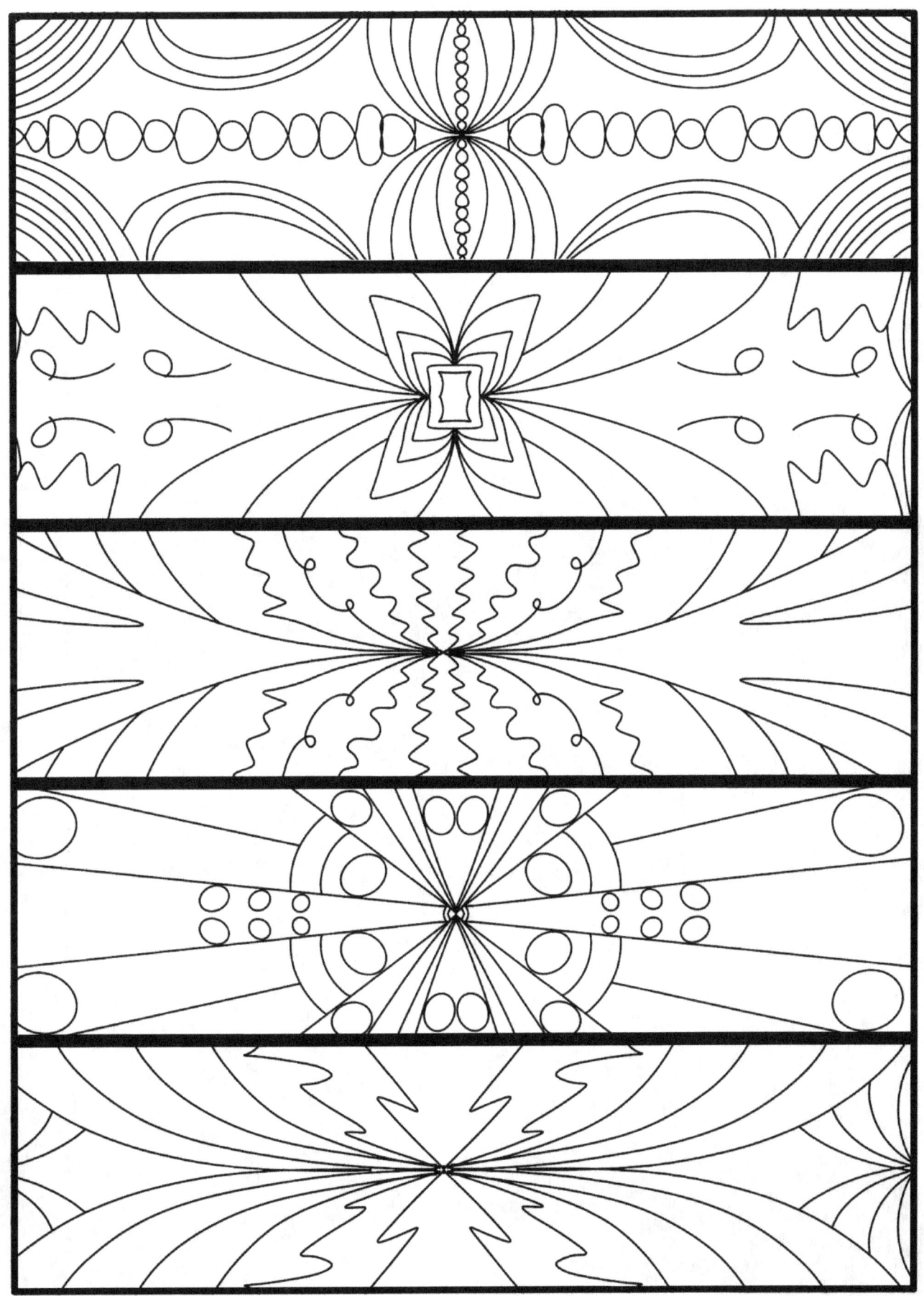

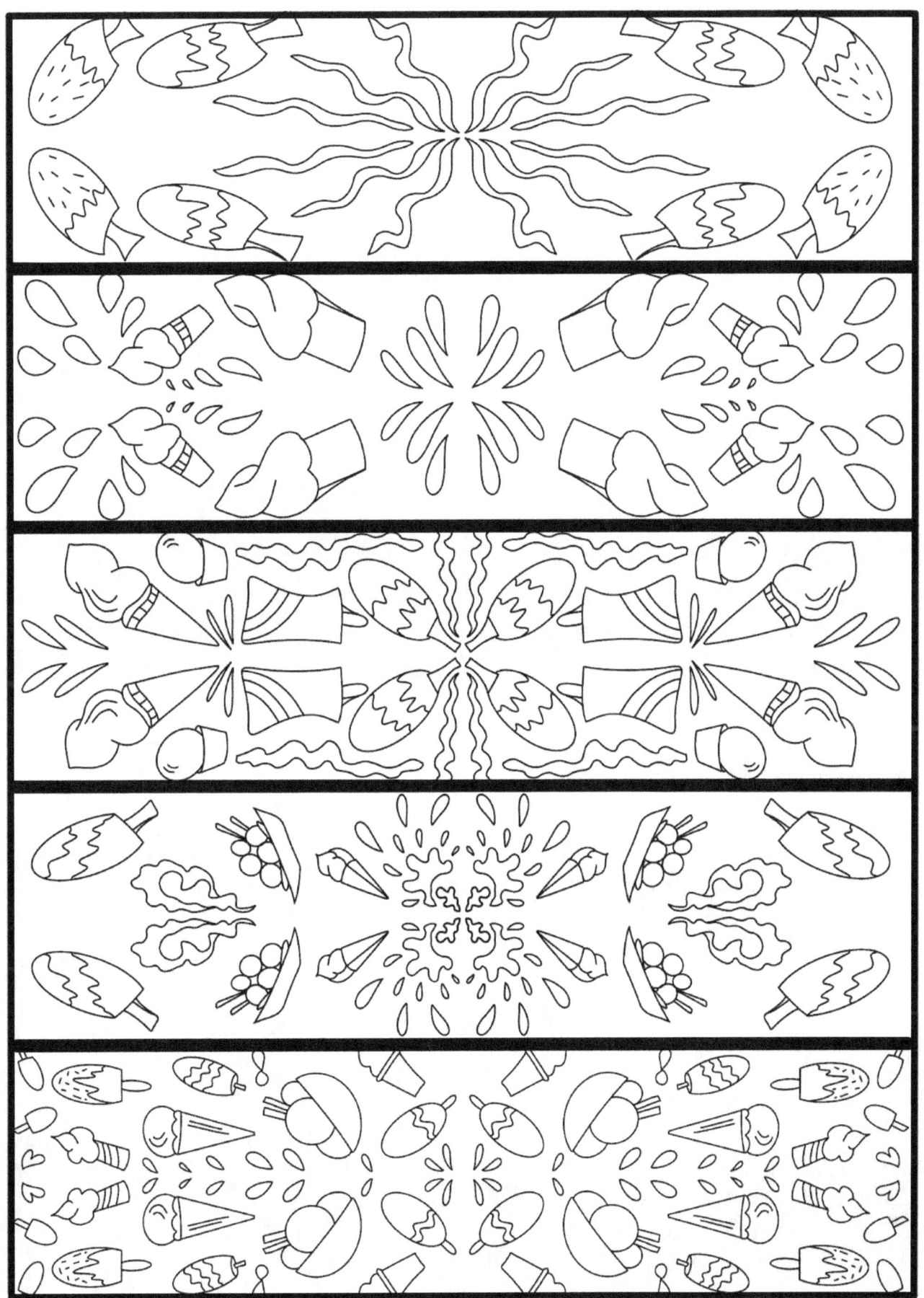

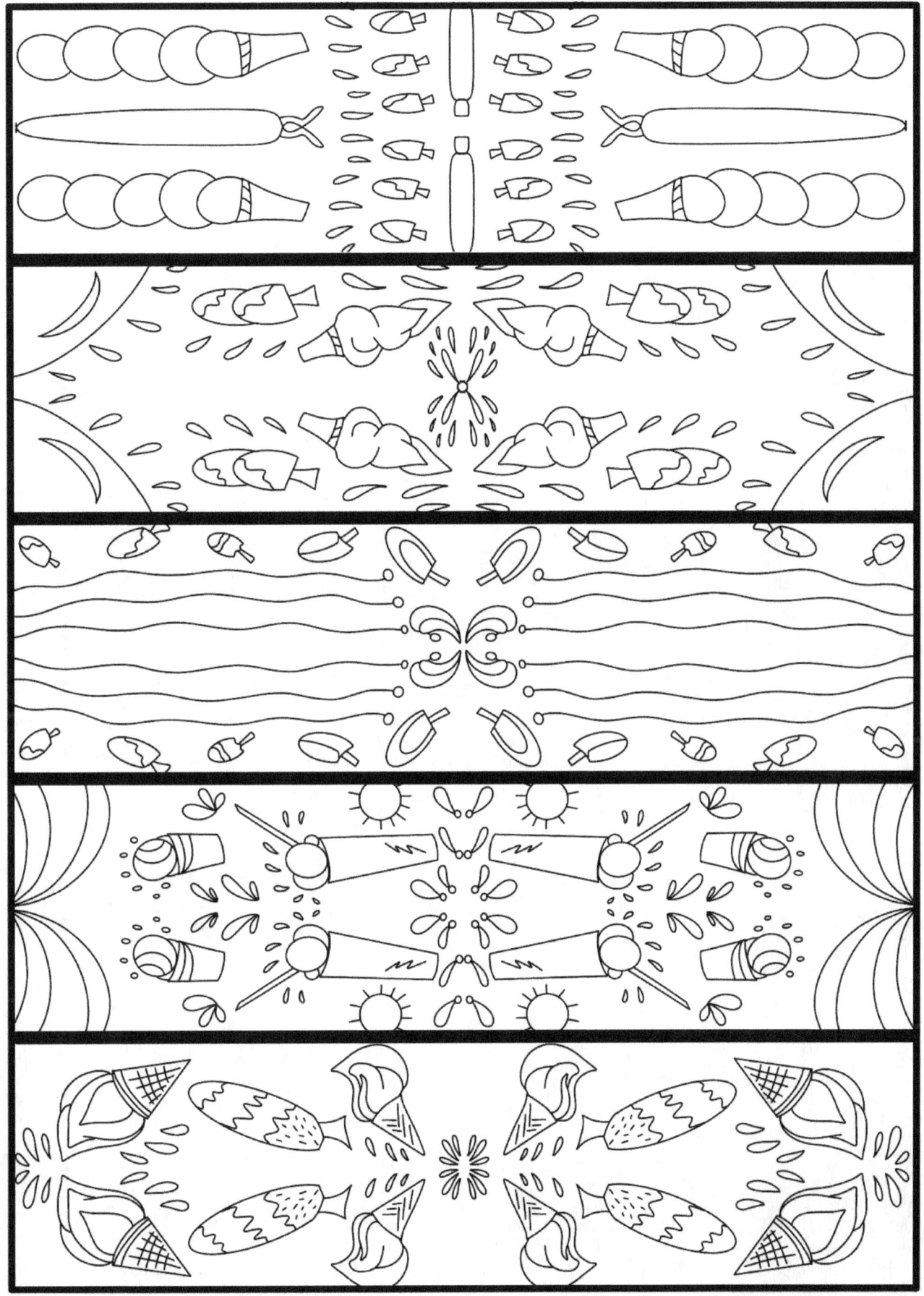

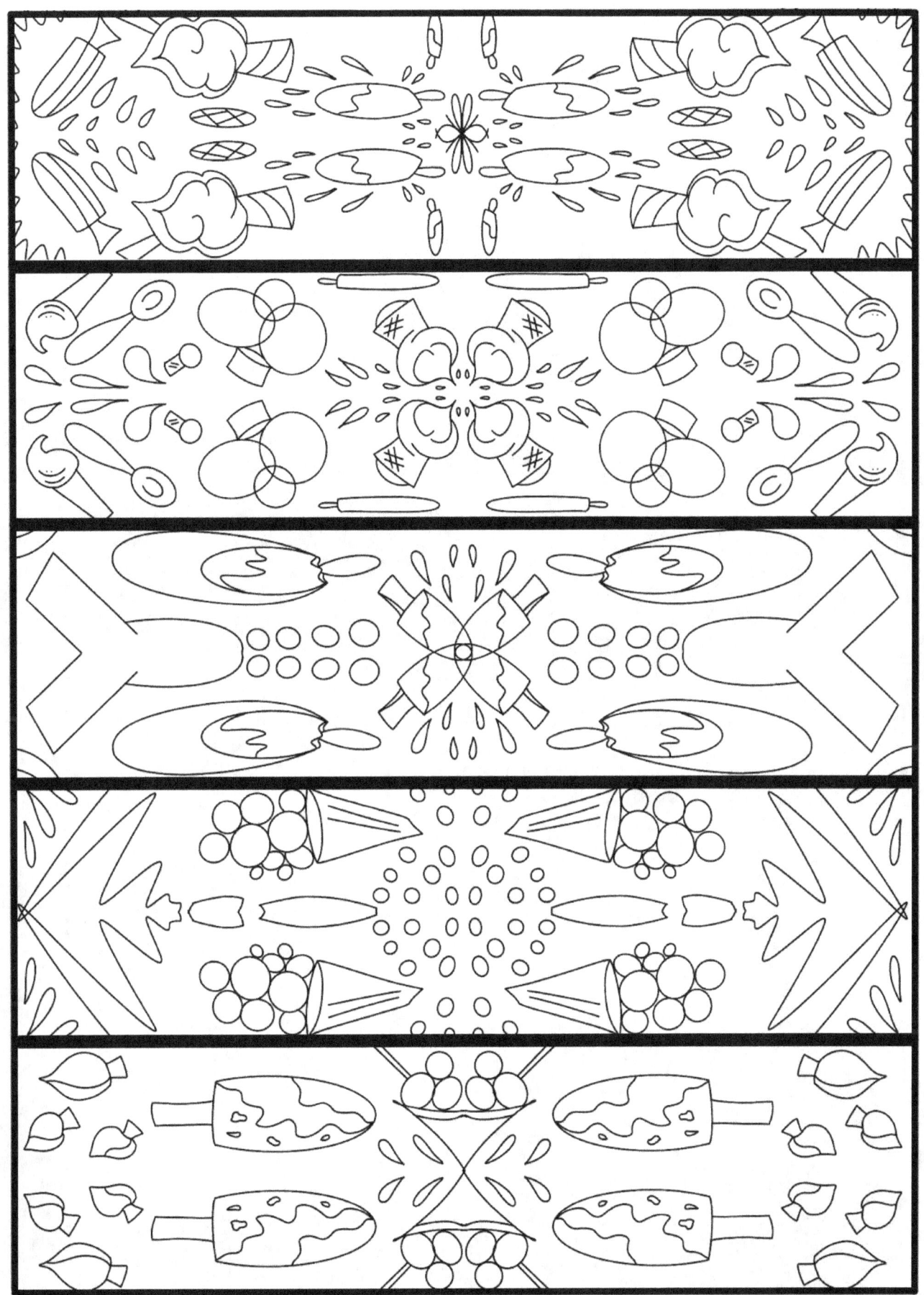

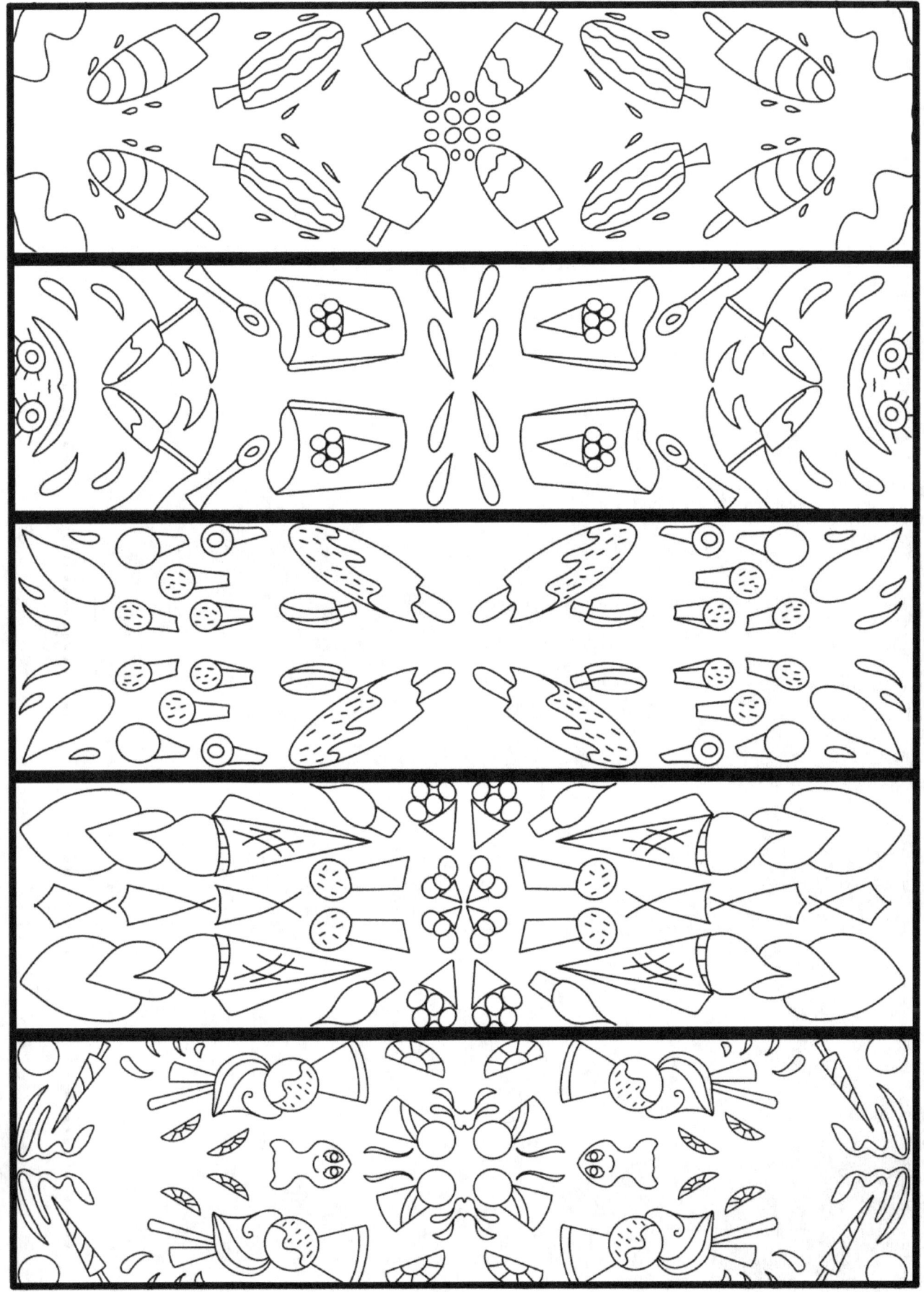

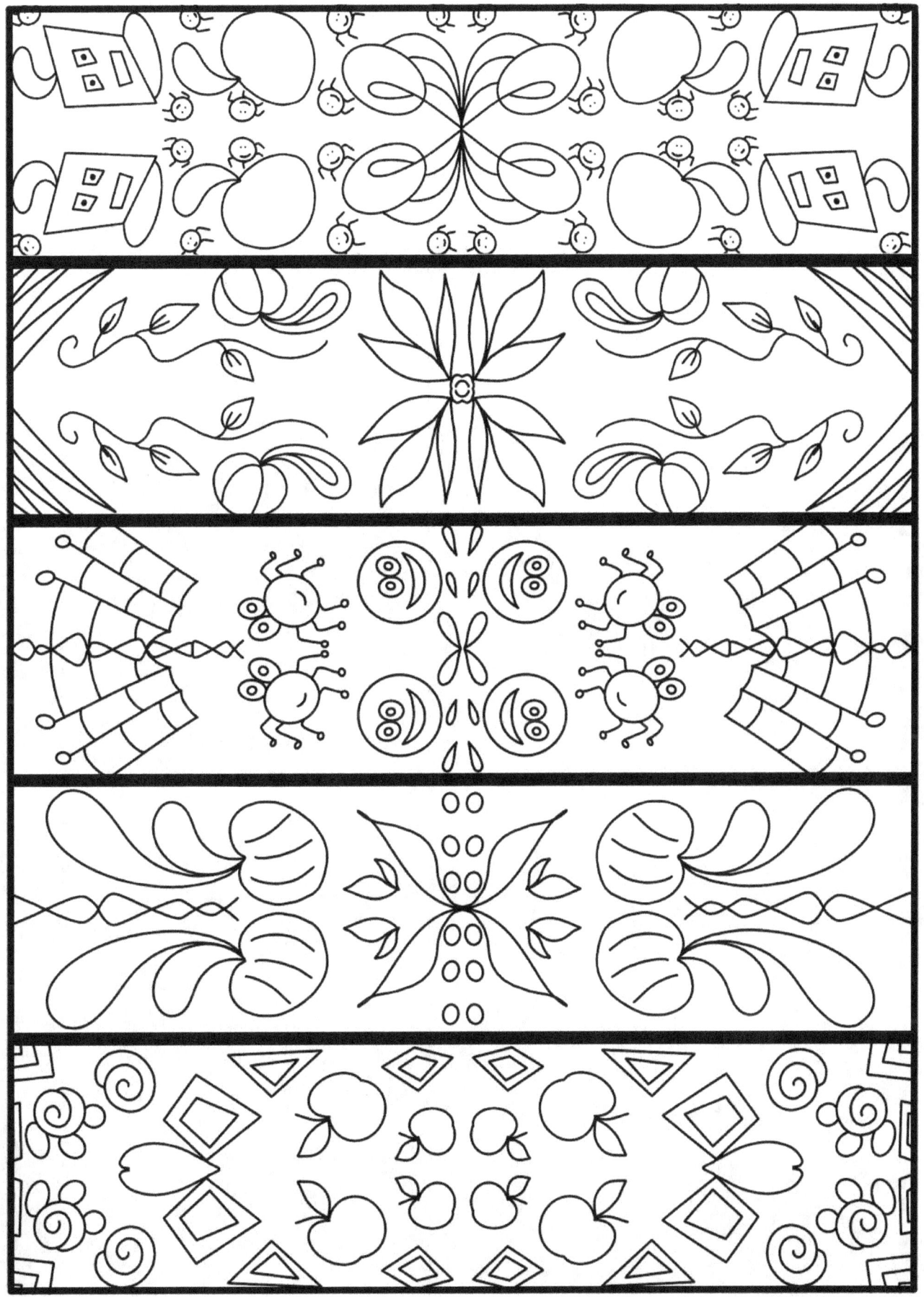

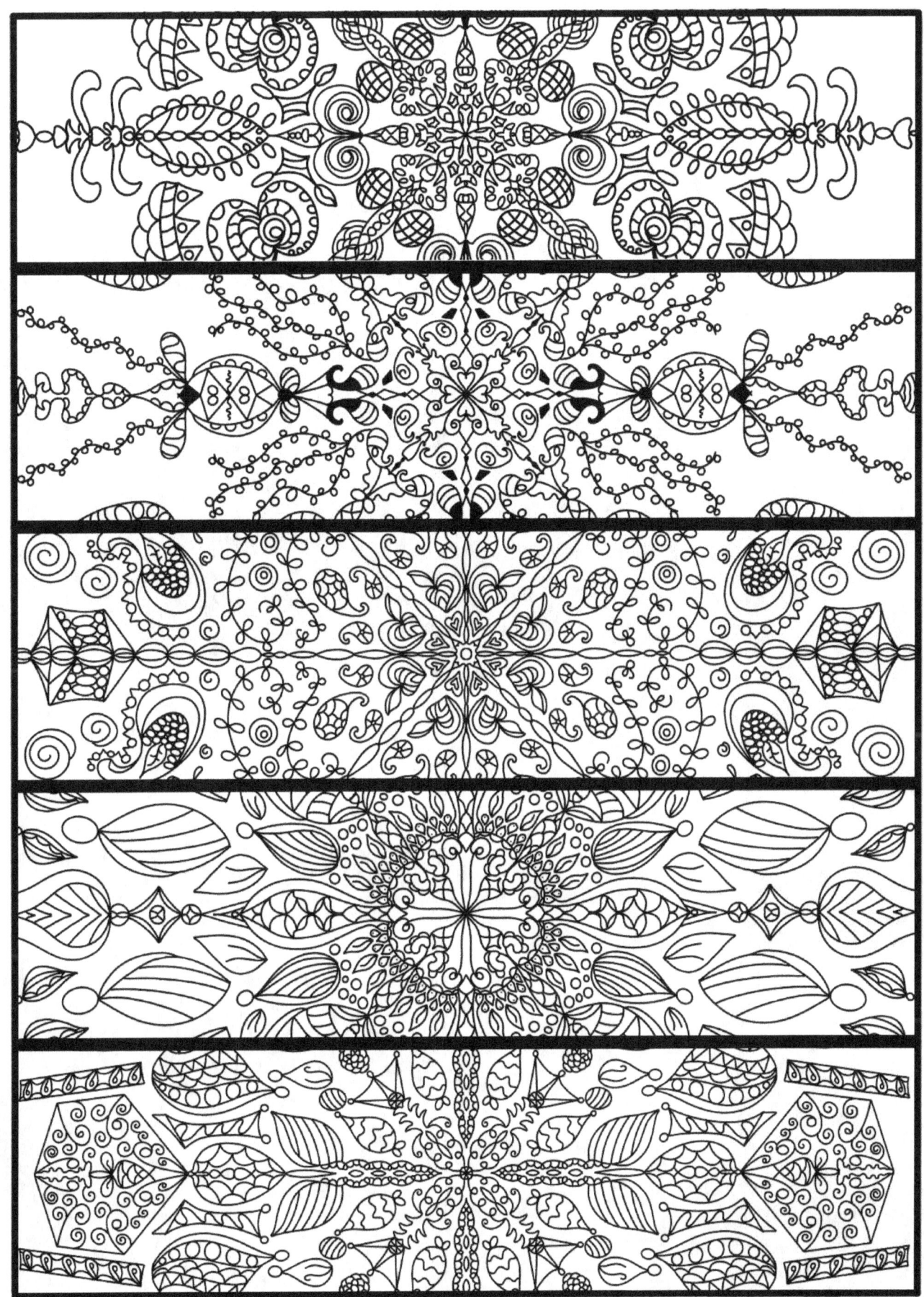

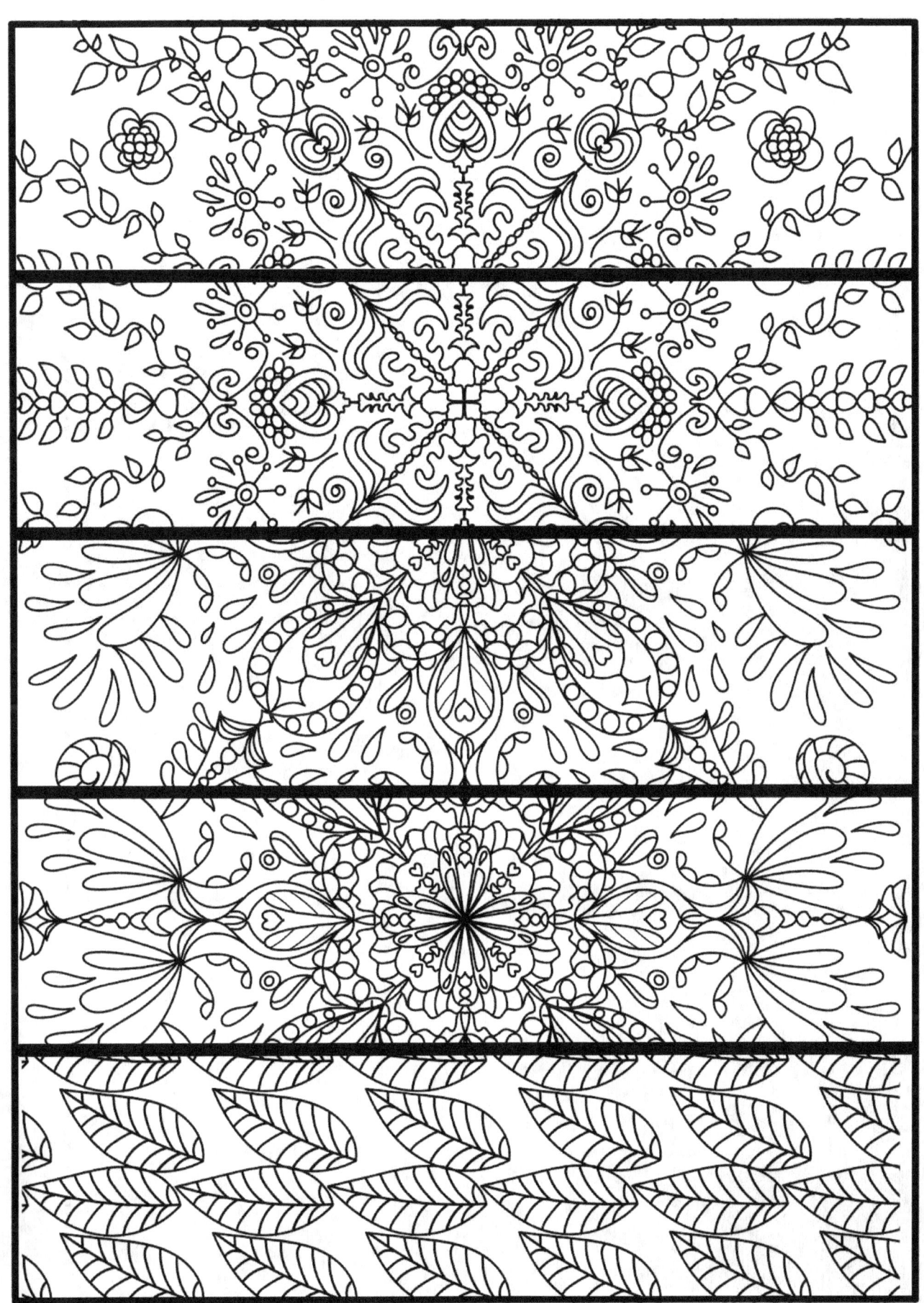

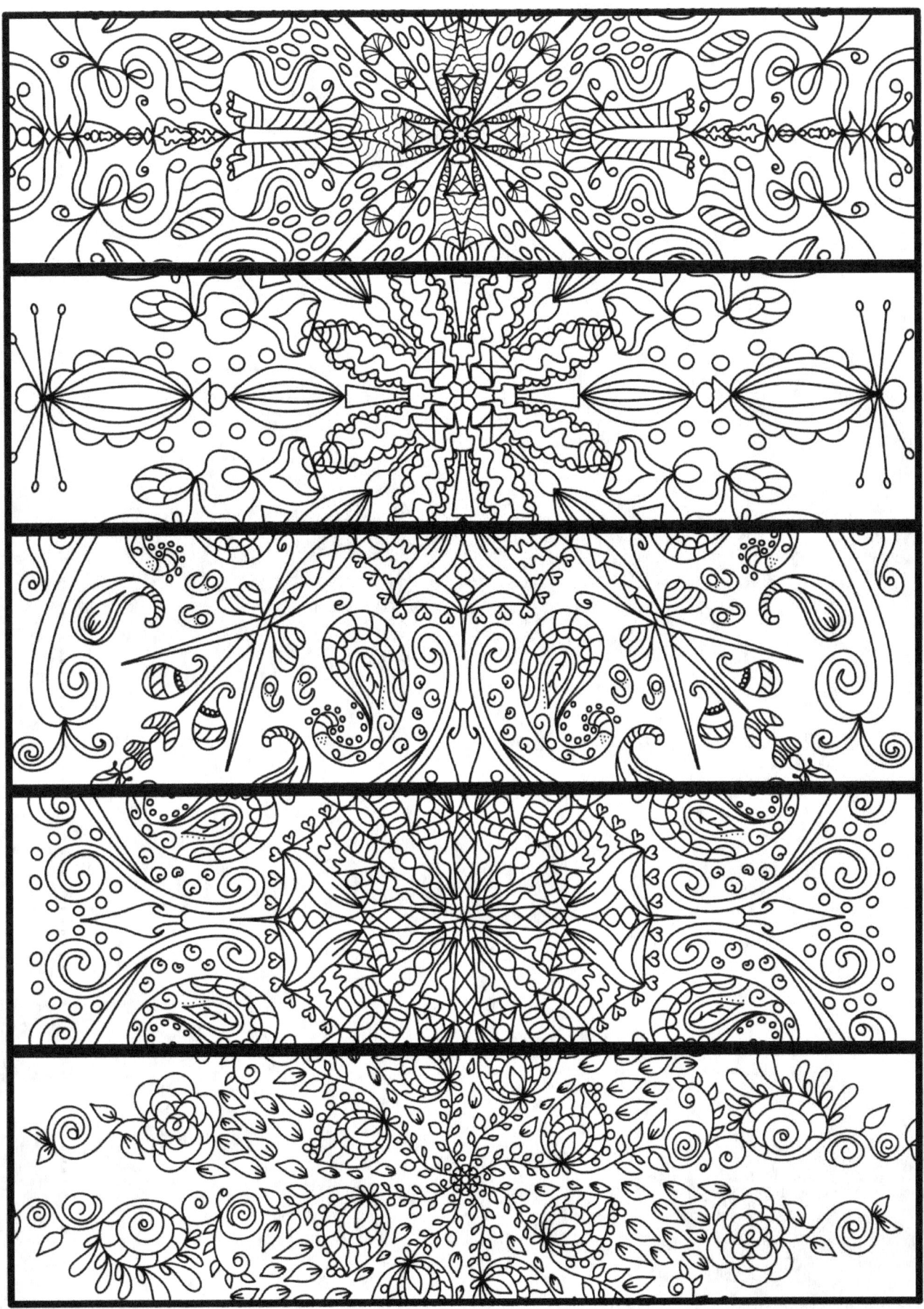

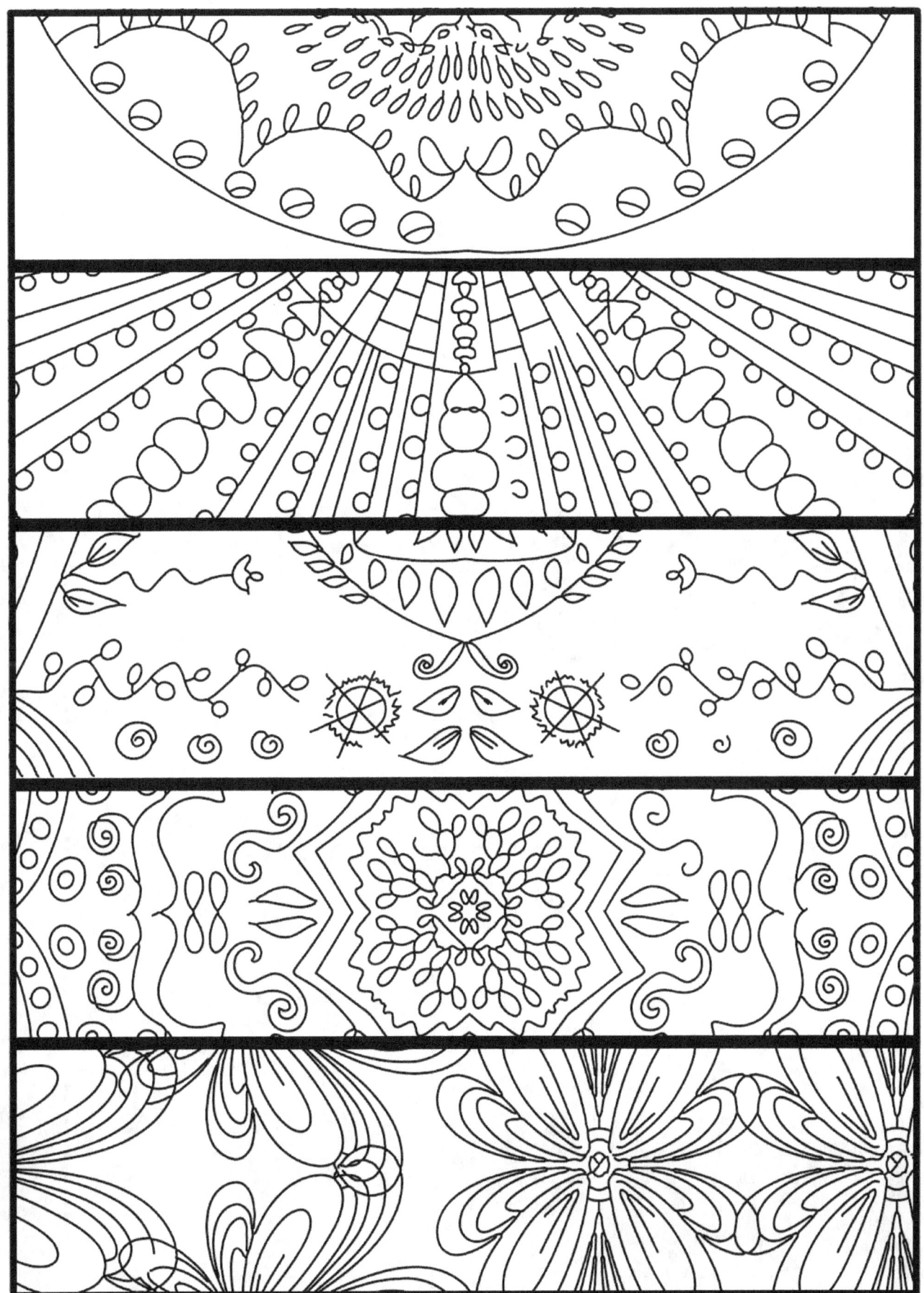

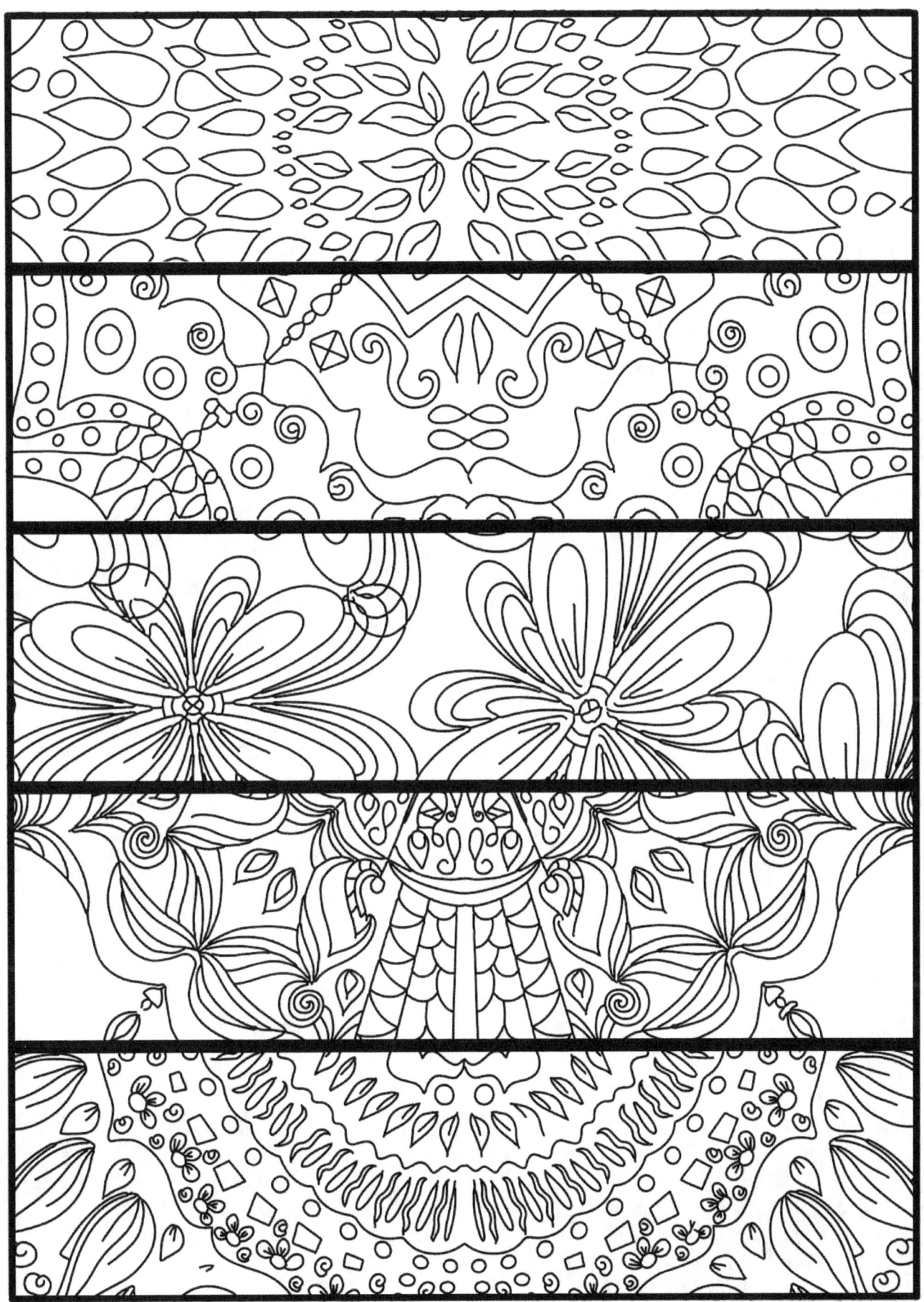

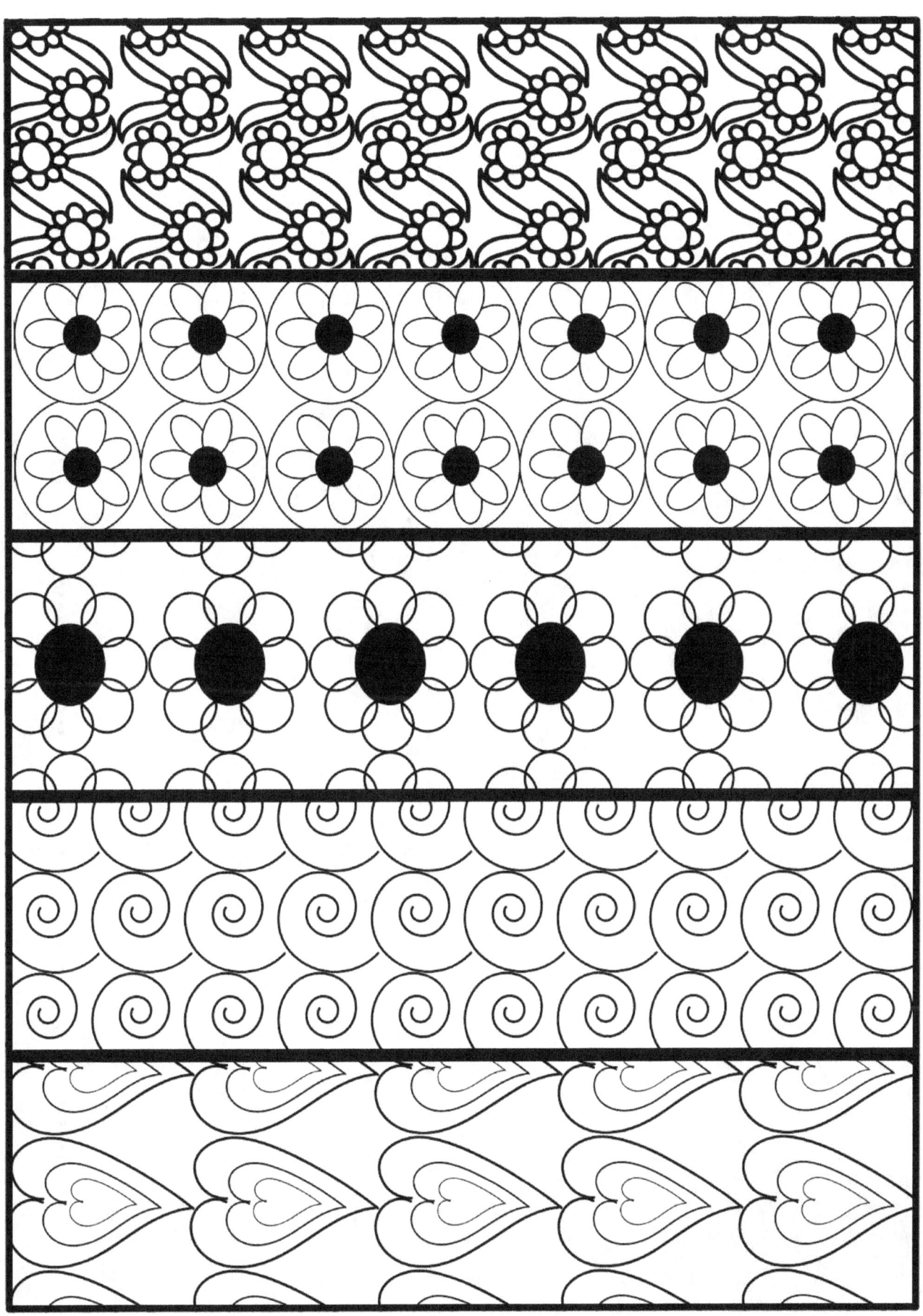

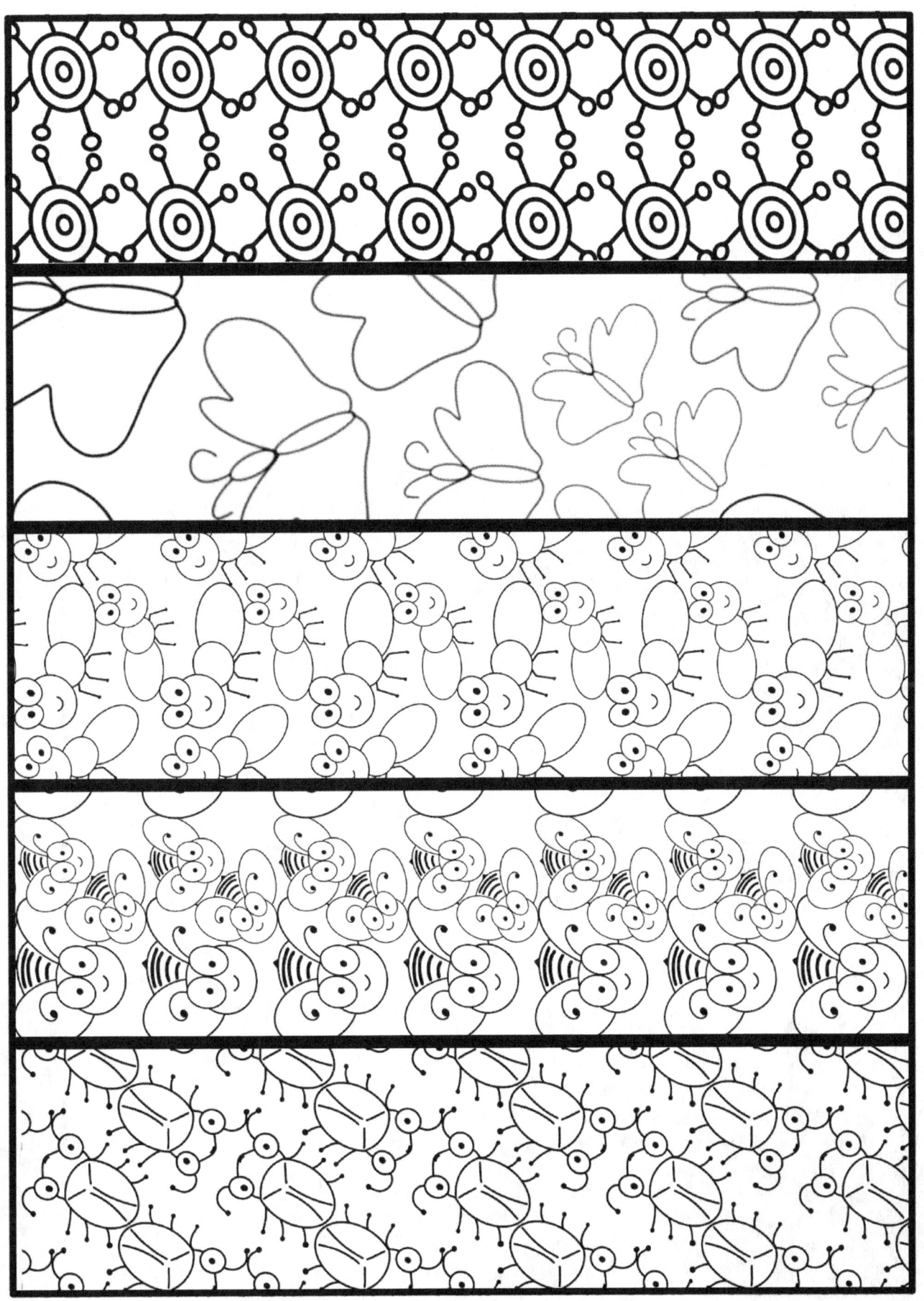

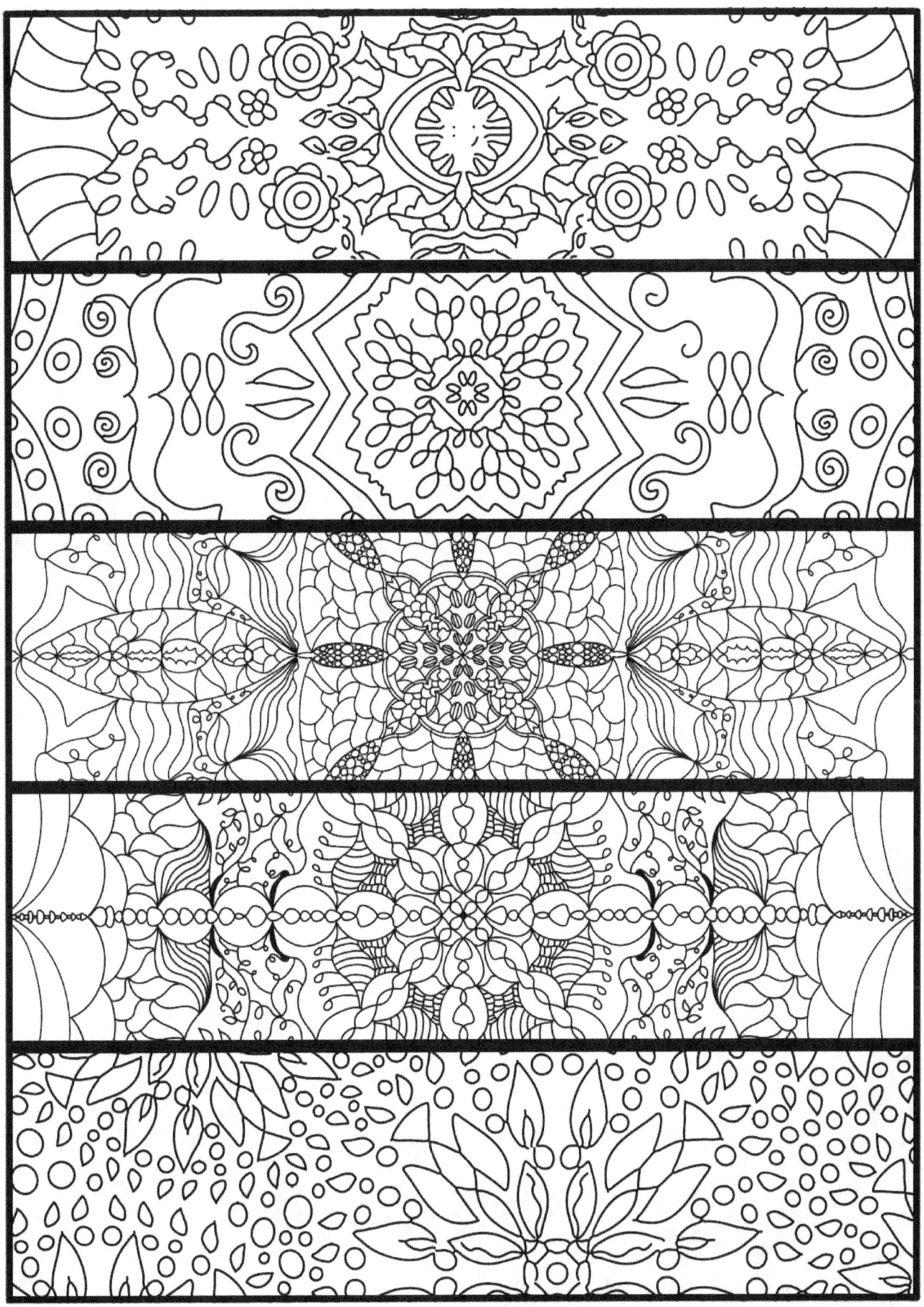

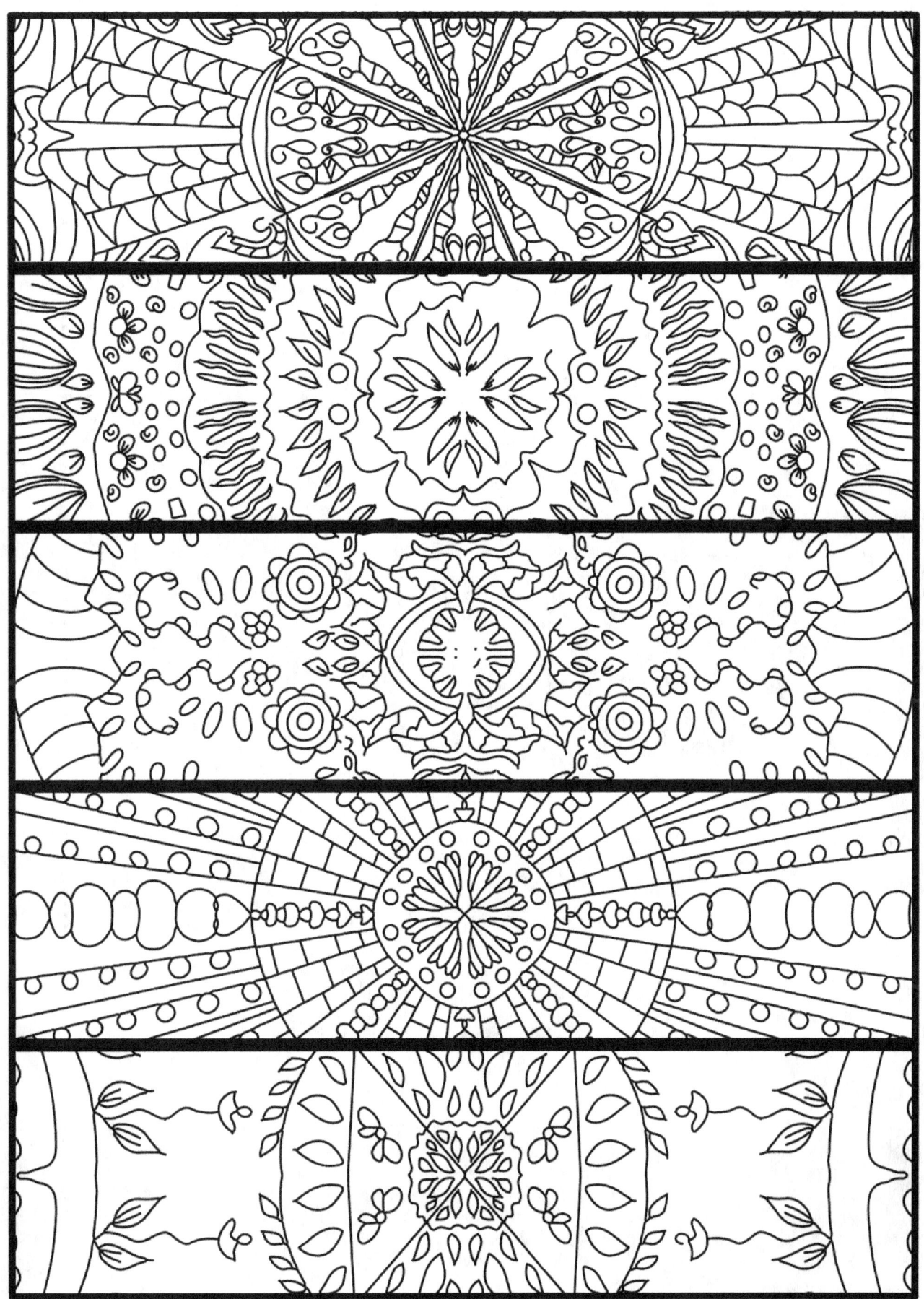

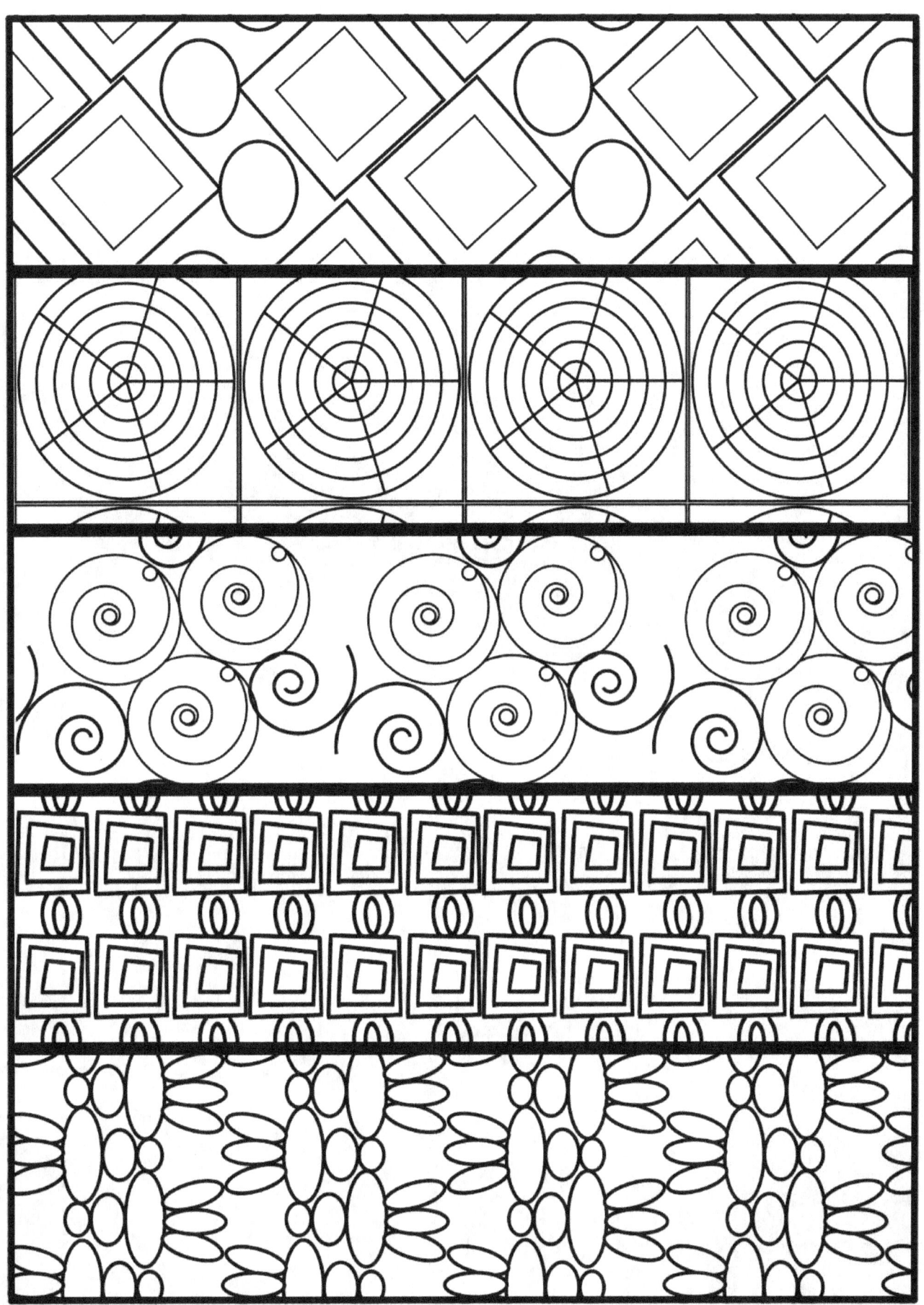

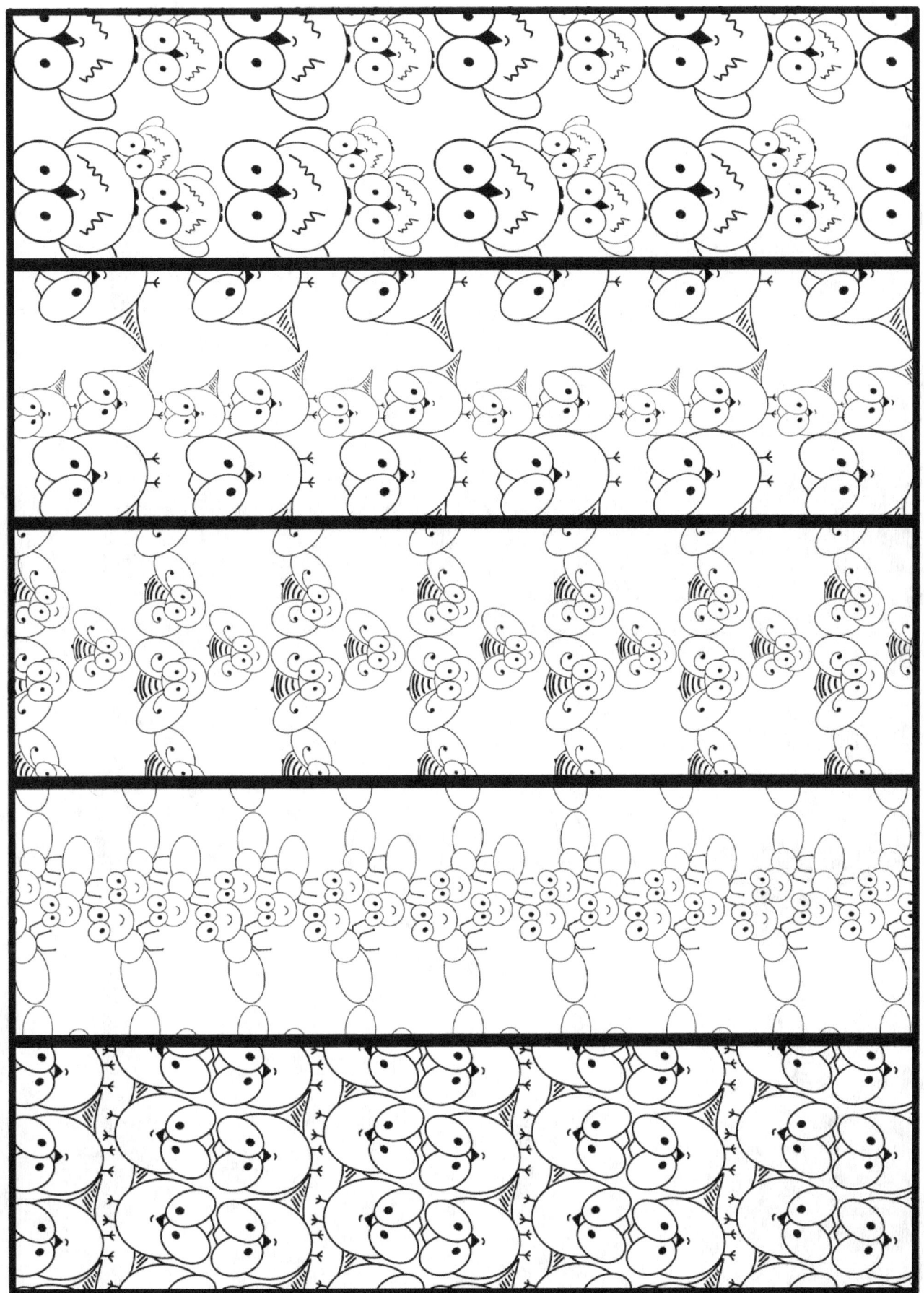

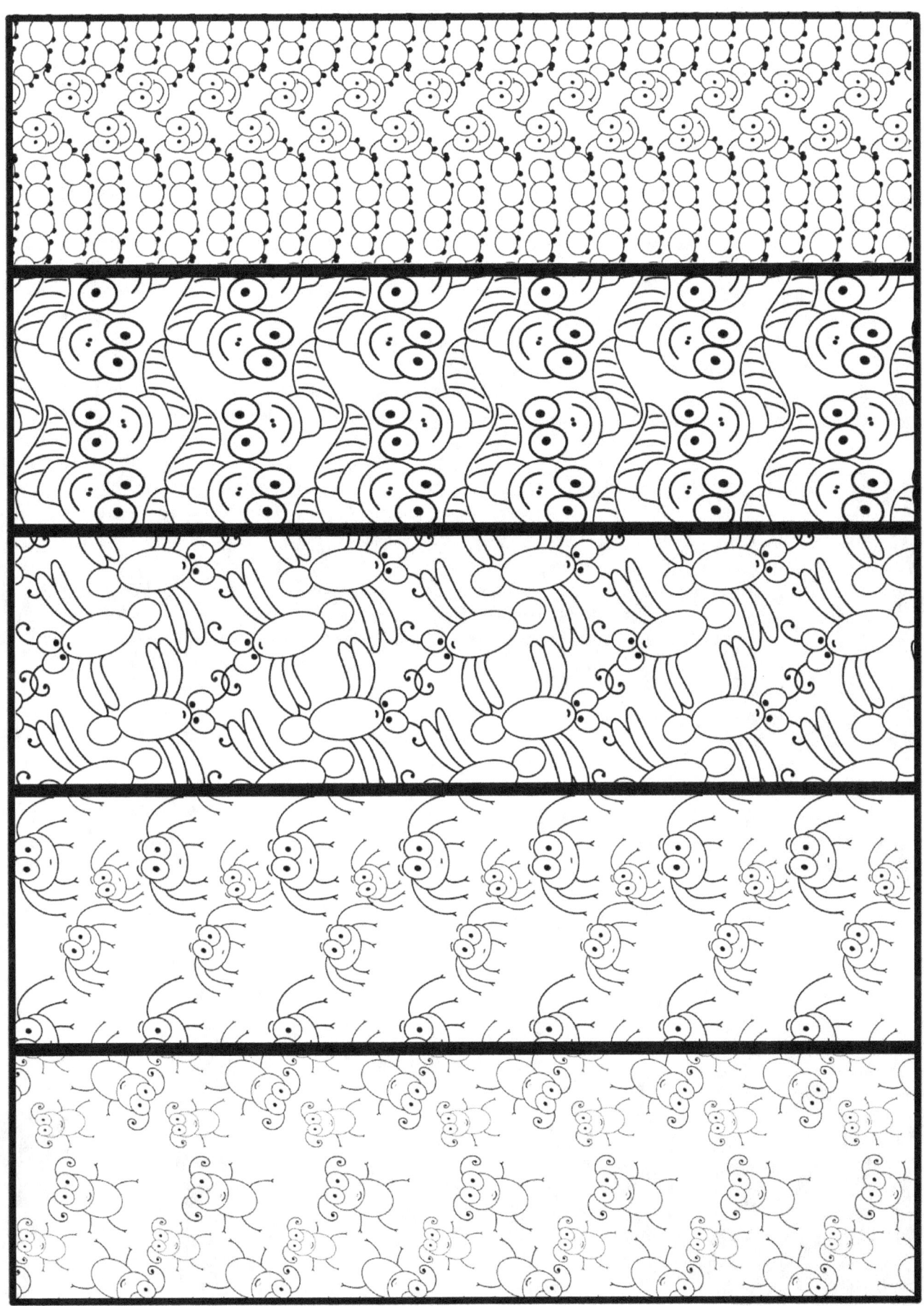